This journal belongs to

Harper Heaney (949-966-3144)

About this journal...

'What we suppress haunts us, what we express frees us'

There is a need in each of us to be heard and to express what we think and feel without censorship or fear of upsetting anyone. Love, joy, hate, anger, fear, confusion, doubt, desire, hopes, dreams, prayers and affirmations are all part of being human; they are valid aspects of who we are. The life force that flows through us is a river of creative energy that generates feelings, emotions and ideas which need to be expressed. If we try to suppress or control the flow, we become creatively and energetically blocked, and if the blockage continues for a significant amount of time it may also affect us physically.

Self-expression is healing. It is a natural and necessary part of leading a healthy, balanced and creative life. There are many ways in which you can express yourself safely without upsetting anyone. It is up to you to choose whatever feels comfortable. Drawing, writing, dancing, talking, screaming, painting, singing, running naked through a forest or your backyard at midnight are just some of the ways you can express yourself; the list is endless.

Expressing an idea can be the first step in making it a reality. Expressing a creative impulse can be a powerful unleashing of energy that can transform your life. Expressing the river of thoughts, ideas, impressions, feelings and emotions that constantly flows through us is vital. Where there is no flow, there is no life or vitality. Prayers can be answered, love can grow, anger can transform to love, healing can occur, clarity can be reached, peace and grace can descend upon us, magic can happen, when we express what is in our hearts and minds.

Expression is the planting of a seed that eventually flowers. This journal can be your flowering – it can be a place where you plant seeds of future creations; a place to collect your scattered thoughts, and express your heart's deepest desires or concerns. It can be a mirror that reflects your unique brilliance and the light and essence of your soul. It can also be a place where light is cast upon your shadow. There is possibly no safer way of expressing yourself than through this journal. And, there are no rules, except for this one: THIS JOURNAL IS FOR YOU AND ONLY YOU. It is important that you feel free to express what you want in any way you want.

Affirmations

The following affirmations are about your connection to this journal. They can be very helpful and powerful if you repeat them, perhaps on a daily basis for a while. I also encourage you to create your own.

Affirmations:

I will spontaneously express all I think, imagine and feel within these pages, without censorship or judgment, in any way I choose. I will honour, love and value everything I express in this journal in the knowing that all is, in essence, light pouring out from my heart.

*

This journal is my sanctuary, a place I go to relax and just be. There is no right or wrong here; there is only love pouring out of my soul. There is nothing about me that I need to fix or change; I love and accept every part of me as I am. There is an infinite ocean of creation inside me. The universe is expressing endless love through me. There is vast space inside my heart, creative energy without beginning or end. I AM ALL THAT I AM. I am a particle of light, I am life, I am devoid of space and time, I am space and time, I am one with all, I am duality also.

*

These pages are a fertile field where I plant my imaginings, thoughts, hopes and dreams. They will be an exploration, a celebration, a meditation, a sacred journey. I am blessed by an outpouring of inner light which helps me see through illusion and perceived faults. I let go of judgment and the need to label things as good, bad, beautiful, ugly, right or wrong. I look within and see the perfection of life. Beyond all thought and suffering there is only love – a vast ocean of love.

Creativity

A thought on that which is beyond thought.

For many years, I held workshops on intuitive art and writing. The people who attended were of all ages and backgrounds. Many of them were initially very timid and seemed afraid of not measuring up to either their own or others' expectations. But their fears dissolved as they realised the workshop was not about performance or producing anything. I made it clear that the workshop had nothing to do with artistic or writing talent. It was not about techniques or formulas, it was simply about self-expression and self-discovery. The only requirement was to be open and not judge anything or anyone, especially themselves. I realised that when people feel safe, accepted and loved, the protective amour melts away and their inner essence shines through.

I discovered that everyone is creative, and everyone is a channel for creativity to flow through. Creativity is life force, and we all have it. It may sound strange, but I'm convinced that the major obstacle to creativity is thinking. Thinking and reasoning block the flow of creativity because, a bit like a computer, the mind, when engaged in thinking and reasoning, can only process pre-existing data – it can only drag up what has already been. Creativity, on the other hand, is a living energy; it is infinite, it is always from the unknown, always arriving for the very first time, fresh and new. It created everything we see around us. The greatest artists who ever lived did not possess any more creativity than you or I. They simply realised that creativity is an energy; a force greater than themselves, and they found ways of allowing that energy through with minimal interference.

You can learn how to draw, paint, write, dance, sing or play a musical instrument, but you cannot learn creativity. It is something you already are and have; all you need is to allow it through without prior analysis or thought. It is that simple, just allow it to be what it wants to be and not what you think it should be. Try it, practice this, and it will surprise you. You will discover that creativity is a wild, super-intelligent force with a heart and mind of its own. It doesn't need you to figure it out or think it into being. It doesn't need you to understand it, manipulate, master or control it. It just needs you to allow it. It has already created an infinite amount of things, like the universe, every form, colour and texture, so trust and let it show you the way – it does have a lot of experience in this area.

With love and blessings,

Toni

1st Cycle -
Started: Sunday, 7/17/22
ended: thursday, 7/21/22

"I have no special talents. I am only passionately curious."
– Albert Einstein

I am changing as I write these words and you are changing as you read them. Even so, there is something inside us that is forever unchanging.

"Do not go where the path may lead, go instead where there is no path and leave a trail." – Ralph Waldo Emerson

Feel it all around you, feel it inside you,
an infinite, all-embracing and creative field of love.

"Fall seven times, stand up eight."
– Japanese Proverb

Love fills every atom of my being with the same love
that moves the earth and stars.

"All know that the drop merges into the ocean,
but few know that the ocean merges into the drop." – Kabir

I tune out of all the noise and confusion of this world,
and tune into a space of infinite peace and love inside my heart.

"The Cosmic Director has written His own plays, and assembled the tremendous casts for the pageant of the centuries. From the dark booth of eternity, He pours His creative beam through the films of successive ages, and the pictures are thrown on the screen of space. Just as the motion-picture images appear to be real, but are only combinations of light and shade, so is the universal variety a delusive seeming. The planetary spheres, with their countless forms of life, are naught but figures in a cosmic motion picture, temporarily true to five sense perceptions as the scenes are cast on the screen of man's consciousness by the infinite creative beam."

– Paramahansa Yogananda

Love is always present for my true nature is love.

"Let there be spaces in your togetherness and let the winds of the heavens dance between you. Love one another but make not a bond of love: let it rather be a moving sea between the shores of your souls." — Khalil Gibran

There is no better time than now to go within. There is no time but now.

"Many of life's failures are experienced by people who did not realize how close they were to success when they gave up." – Thomas Edison

A powerful creative force flows through my heart, mind and thoughts.
I am one with all creation.

"I believe a leaf of grass is no less than the journey work of the stars."
– Walt Whitman

I am light.

"What you seek is seeking you."

– Rumi

The Goddess of Creation dwells in my heart.

"Success is not final, failure is not fatal —
it is the courage to continue that counts." – Winston Churchill

Just beyond the surface of this human drama
there is a space of infinite love.

"A mighty flame follows a tiny spark." – Dante

"*Look deep into nature, and then you will understand everything better.*"
– Albert Einstein

Eternity is a very long time and yet it is also no time at all.

"The artist is a receptacle for emotions that come from all over the place: from the sky, from the earth, from a scrap of paper, from a passing shape, from a spider's web." – Pablo Picasso

*I rise above the transient thoughts of this world
and enter a crystal clear space of light.*

"In the end, it's not going to matter how many breaths you took, but how many moments took your breath away." – Shing Xiong

Creativity flows through me like a river.
I am a channel, an expression of its love.

"I bequeath myself to the dirt to grow from the grass I love."
– Walt Whitman

We travel through endless corridors within our mind
until we find a path that leads to the heart.

"A wound is the place where light enters you." – Rumi

Your spirit is ageless and timeless.
You are a timeless soul in a world of imaginary time.

"This world is one drop in an infinite ocean, one link in an infinite chain."
– Swami Vivekananda

Divine Mother forever present in my heart, renewing, destroying, building, transforming, blessing every moment.

Through the sound of the breeze, through a whisper from a star,
through the spirit of the trees, through a ray of sun,
I feel you

"To be yourself in a world that is constantly trying to make you something
else is the greatest accomplishment." – Albert Einstein

Inside every atom there is endless space.

"Remember always that only the free have free will; all the rest are in bondage and are not responsible for what they do. Will as will is bound. The water when melting on the top of the Himalayas is free, but becoming the river, it is bound by the banks; yet the original impetus carries it to sea and it regains its freedom."

– Swami Vivekananda

Life is without beginning or end, forever changing, forever unchanging.

"The main thing is to be moved, to love, to hope, to tremble, to live."
– Auguste Rodin

A tide of emotion ebbs and flows upon this page.

"If I create from the heart, nearly everything works;
if from the head, almost nothing." – Marc Chagall

I am the author, director and star of a most intriguing play
which is my life.

"The longer you look at an object, the more abstract it becomes, and, ironically, the more real." – Lucian Freud

I am grateful for all that I am and all that is.
Blessed Be.

"The aim of art is to represent not the outward appearance of things,
but their inward significance." – Aristotle

Dreams are the meeting point between the conscious and the unconscious, the merging of heaven and earth.

"Painting is just another way of keeping a diary." – Pablo Picasso

Beyond the crashing waves of thought there is an ocean of infinite peace.

"Art washes away from the soul the dust of everyday life." – Pablo Picasso

"I found I could say things with color and shapes that I couldn't say any other way — things I had no words for." - Georgia O'Keeffe

"If people knew how hard I worked to get my mastery, it wouldn't seem so wonderful at all." – Michelangelo

"Every manifestation of power in the universe is 'Mother.' She is life. She is intelligence. She is love. She is the universe, yet separate from it." – Swami Vivekananda

Sunlight streams through trees, a gentle breeze blows, a leaf falls, and the earth smiles.

"There are only two ways to live your life. One is as though nothing is a miracle. The other is as though everything is a miracle." – Albert Einstein

From within the heart of the earth, many future earths shall be born;
from within the heart of this life, many future lives.

"The calm sea is the Absolute; the same sea in waves is Divine Mother."
– Swami Vivekananda

I feel an ocean of dreams, memories, feelings and emotion,
flow out across these pages.

"To create one's own world takes courage." – Georgia O'Keeffe

Calm the mind and you will find yourself in another dimension.

"The way is perfect like vast space where nothing is lacking and nothing is in excess. Indeed, it is due to our choosing to accept or reject that we do not see the true nature of things." – Sosan

I was once a particle of light; now I am a trillion stars.

"Now I see the secret of making the best person:
it is to grow in the open air and to eat and sleep with the earth."
– Walt Whitman

Looking forward one million years, all has transformed to light.
I am a body of light, the earth is made of light and all is one through light.

"Through you I drain the pent-up rivers of myself,
in you I wrap a thousand onward years." – Walt Whitman

Change is life's creative flow.

"You exist in time, but you belong to eternity.
You are a penetration of eternity into the world of time.
You are deathless, living in a body of death.
Your consciousness knows no death, no birth.
It is only your body that is born and dies.
But you are not aware of your consciousness.
You are not conscious of your consciousness.
And that is the whole art of meditation;
Becoming conscious of consciousness itself."

– Osho

I am spaceless, I am timeless.

"Keep your face always toward the sunshine —
and shadows will fall behind you." – Walt Whitman

All I feel, I express without judgment or censorship — the good, the bad and the ugly — in the knowing that these are simply labels. All deserves to be loved.

"Darkness cannot drive out darkness: only light can do that.
Hate cannot drive out hate: only love can do that." – Martin Luther King Jr.

The essence of creativity is love
The secret to unlocking creativity is love.

"*Let your soul stand cool and composed before a million universes.*"
– Walt Whitman

I am grateful.

"Where there is hatred, let me sow love; where there is injury, pardon; where there is doubt, faith." – Prayer of St. Francis of Assisi

Today I honour life by expressing how I feel.

"If it's not here it cannot be there." – Swami Vivekananda

Today I honour life by doing something I love.

"The position of the artist is humble. He is essentially a channel."
– Piet Mondrian

A stream of creativity flows from an ocean inside my soul.

"No great artist ever sees things as they really are.
If he did, he would cease to be an artist." – Oscar Wilde

"Mother is the manifestation of power and is considered a higher idea than father.

With the name of mother comes the idea of Sakti, Divine Energy and omnipotence." – Swami Vivekananda

Beyond this mind, that this moment is thinking about what to say or how to say it, there is a higher mind, that says everything without thinking or speaking.

"Everything has its beauty, but not everyone sees it."
– Andy Warhol

Today I accept and love both the positive and negative aspects
of myself and others.

"Creativity is just connecting things. When you ask creative people how they did something, they feel a little guilty because they didn't really do it, the just saw something. It seemed obvious to them after a while."

– Steve Jobs

Today I remember that everything out there is also within me.

"Have no fear of perfection, you'll never reach it." – Salvador Dali

Creativity ebbs and flows in my heart.

"The earth has music for those who listen." – William Shakespeare

The empty space between my thoughts is a gateway to infinite creation.

"The most beautiful thing we can experience is the mysterious.
It is the source of all true art and science." – Albert Einstein

When my dreams become reality I must try to remember that it's all a dream.

"The truth will set you free. But first, it will piss you off." – Gloria Steinem

Sometimes obstacles are a blessing in disguise.

Often, it is through our darkest moments that we come to see things more clearly. When we give in to life and stop trying to control it or make it happen, we find peace and clarity. Life and creativity start to flow again, and we hear that inner voice again.

The light of your soul glows infinite wisdom greater
than all the knowing of this world.

"Great things are done by a series of small things brought together."
— Vincent Van Gogh

Follow your own guidance and don't let your plans and dreams be crushed by the opinions of others.

"Nature is not only all that is visible to the eye...
it also includes the inner pictures of the soul." – Edvard Munch

Ultimately all of creation is one. Division exists only in the mind.

"One can have no smaller or greater mastery than mastery of oneself."
– Leonardo da Vinci

The dark fertile void of creation is a mystery yearning to be filled.
Darkness and light are intertwined; one is always flowing to the other.

"Every child is an artist. The problem is how to remain an artist once he grows up." – Pablo Picasso

Let this world be a playground for your soul.

"The greater the artist, the greater the doubt. Perfect confidence is granted to the less talented as a consolation prize." – Robert Hughes

Life is the unfolding of divinity.

"I dream of painting and then I paint my dream." – Vincent Van Gogh

Connect, see and feel the infinite beauty.

"When I say artist I mean the one who is building things...some with a brush — some with a shovel — some choose a pen." – Jackson Pollock

Light and dark are both aspects of you. Accept and love all that you perceive to be good or bad about you. Love all equally, and make no distinction between one or another, for all is a valuable part of you.

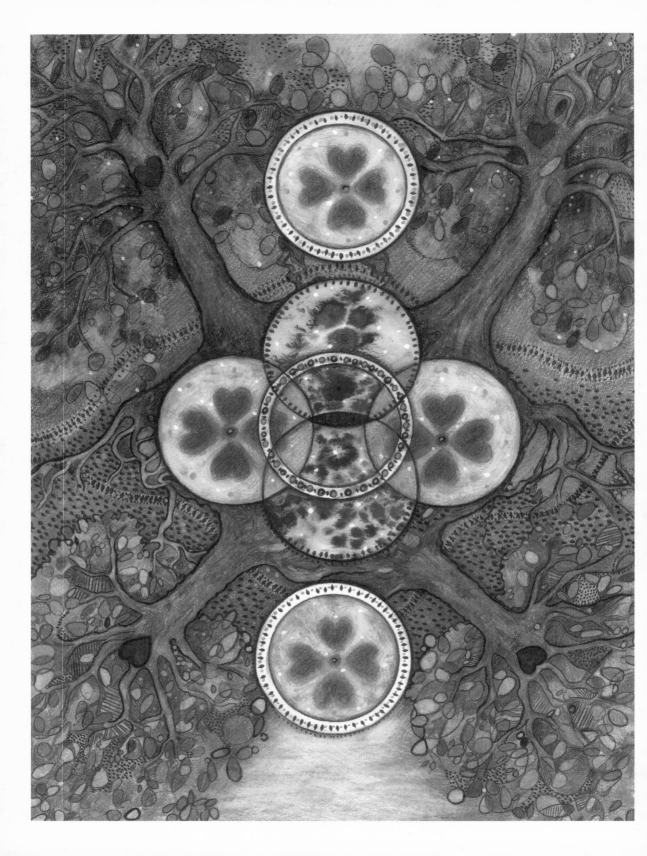

If you need a mission, let it be to love the world. This does not mean that you make no effort to help change things. It simply means that you do everything you do lovingly.

"The most common way people give up their power is by thinking they don't have any." – Alice Walker

Creativity is like your inner child. Unless it feels safe and loved,
it won't come out and play.

"Do not be satisfied with the stories that come before you.
Unfold your own myth." – Rumi

This life is beyond understanding, words or description.
We exist, we are alive, we observe, we dream.

"Creativity is intelligence having fun."
– Albert Einstein

Your imagination is your creative centre.

"All I can be is me — whoever that is."

– Bob Dylan

When people ask me where I get my inspiration from I answer, "From life."
Where else could I get it from?

"Paint the flying spirit of the bird rather than its feathers."
– Robert Henri

Through the eye of the soul all is perfect.

"Weeds are flowers, too, once you get to know them."
– A.A. Milne

Acknowledge what you feel in your heart;
know that no dream is too great within this cosmic dream of life.

"The Great Way is not difficult for those who have no preferences.
When love and hate are both absent everything becomes clear and
undisguised. Make the smallest distinction, however, and heaven
and earth are set infinitely apart."

– Sosan

Only through darkness can we see the stars above us.

"The most beautiful people we have known are those who have known defeat, known suffering, known struggle, known loss, and have found their way out of the depths." – Elizabeth Kubler Ross

Love yourself unconditionally — every part of you, just as you are, without trying to change any part of yourself. Forget about who you could or should become and know that you are perfect just as you are this moment.

"Faith is taking the first step even when you can't see the whole staircase."
– Martin Luther King Jr.

If something doesn't feel right then it's not right for me.

"Always be on the lookout for the presence of wonder."

– E.B. White

Today I will not stress.

"Every artist dips his brush in his own soul, and paints his own nature into his pictures." – Henry Ward Beecher

The Universe is alive and listening and responding.

"The only journey is the one within." - Rainer Maria Rilke

It takes no more effort to dream big than to dream small.

"Fill your paper with the breathings of your heart." – William Wordsworth

"To draw, you must close your eyes and sing." – Pablo Picasso

"Art is when you hear a knocking from your soul — and you answer."
– Terri Guillemets

Every statement we make is both right and wrong unless followed by an opposite contradictory statement. Nothing is completely right or wrong. Realising that life is full of contradiction is the first step to mastering it.

Creativity is the life force within everything.
Even a stone is creative because every atom of it is full of life.

"Our lives begin to end the day we become silent about things that matter."
– Martin Luther King Jr.

When the mind is not at war with the heart, there is peace.

"Don't let the noise of others' opinions drown out your own inner voice. And most important, have the courage to follow your heart and intuition. They somehow already know what you truly want to become."

– Steve Jobs

Today I love and accept the world as it is.

"I have no special talents. I am only passionately curious."
– Albert Einstein

Express the inexpressible.
Release the uncontainable and untamed part of you.

"If you hear a voice within you say, 'You cannot paint,' then by all means paint, and that voice will be silenced." – Vincent Van Gogh

Creativity is a mystery which cannot be understood.
It can be erratic and wild or calm and full of infinite peace.
Creativity is life expressing itself through you.

"Re-examine all you have been told. Dismiss what insults your soul."
– Walt Whitman

A million years from now the same light glows in my heart and the
the same love glows in my soul.

"We must accept finite disappointment, but we must never lose infinite hope."
– Martin Luther King

Something inside you is glowing brighter.
Something is healing, shifting, unfolding, transforming.

"Be yourself — not your idea of what you think somebody else's idea of yourself should be." – Henry David Thoreau

Love is the only thing we take with us.